DISCOVER AND DO!

HISTORY

ANCIENT EGYPTIANS

Written by Jane Lacey

Enslow PUBLISHING

Published in 2024 by Enslow Publishing, LLC
2544 Clinton Street
Buffalo, NY 14224

Editor: Izzi Howell
Designer: Clare Nicholas
Series designer: Rocket Design (East Anglia) Ltd

Manufactured in the United States of America

CPSIA compliance information: Batch #CW24ENS: For further information contact
Enslow Publishing LLC, New York, New York at 1-800-398-2504.

Please visit our website, www.enslowpublishing.com. For a free color catalog of all our high-quality books,
call toll free 1-800-398-2504 or fax 1-877-980-4454.

Cataloging-in-Publication Data

Names: Lacey, Jane.
Title: Ancient Egyptians / Jane Lacey.
Description: New York : Enslow Publishing, 2024. | Series: Discover and do: history | Includes glossary and index.
Identifiers: ISBN 9781978538238 (pbk.) | ISBN 9781978538245 (library bound) | ISBN 9781978538252 (ebook)
Subjects: LCSH: Egypt--Civilization--To 332 B.C.--Juvenile literature. | Egypt--History--To 332 B.C.--Juvenile literature.
Classification: LCC DT61.L33 2024 | DDC 932'.01--dc23

Picture credits:
t=top b=bottom m=middle l=left r=right

Getty: ikryannikovgmailcom 6l and 29b, PeterHermesFurian 8t, SSPL 23t, Abrill_ 24t; The Metropolitan Museum of Art: Rogers Fund, 1908 15t, Rogers Fund and Edward S. Harkness Gift, 1920 16b, Rogers Fund, 1934 21t; Shutterstock: cover and title page Elegant Solution, klyaksun 4, 5tr, 22b and 31t, GoodStudio 5tl and 14b, OlgaChernyak 5b and 18, vectorpouch 6r, Olga Kuevda 7t, 8b and 31b, Cortyn 10t and 32, tan_tan 10b, matrioshka 11, Federico Rostagno 12t, HappyPictures 12b, Dario Lo Presti 16t and 30t, Lars Poyansky 17t and 29t, Liudmila Klymenko 20t, PremiumStock 20bl and 28, Ashwin 20br, Eroshka 22t, Pavel Kukol 24b, Eugene Li 25t, Love Lego 26l, Colin Hayes 26r and 31c; Walters Art Museum: Acquired by Henry Walters, 1909 14t and 30b.

All design elements from Shutterstock.
Craft models from a previous series made by Anna-Marie D'Cruz/photos by Steve Shott.

DISCOVER AND DO!

HISTORY

ANCIENT EGYPTIANS

Written by Jane Lacey

Enslow PUBLISHING

CONTENTS

Words that appear in **bold** can be found in the glossary on pages 28–29.

THE EGYPTIANS

The Ancient Egyptians lived near the banks of the Nile River in Egypt. There was plenty of water and the soil was good for farming. Their civilization started in 3,100 BCE and ended in 30 BCE when Egypt became part of the Roman Empire.

Egyptian civilization

The Egyptians were ruled by a king called a **pharaoh**. They were clever **engineers** who built cities with magnificent palaces, temples, and **tombs**. The remains of pots, weapons, tools, and jewelry found show that they were also skilled craftsmen.

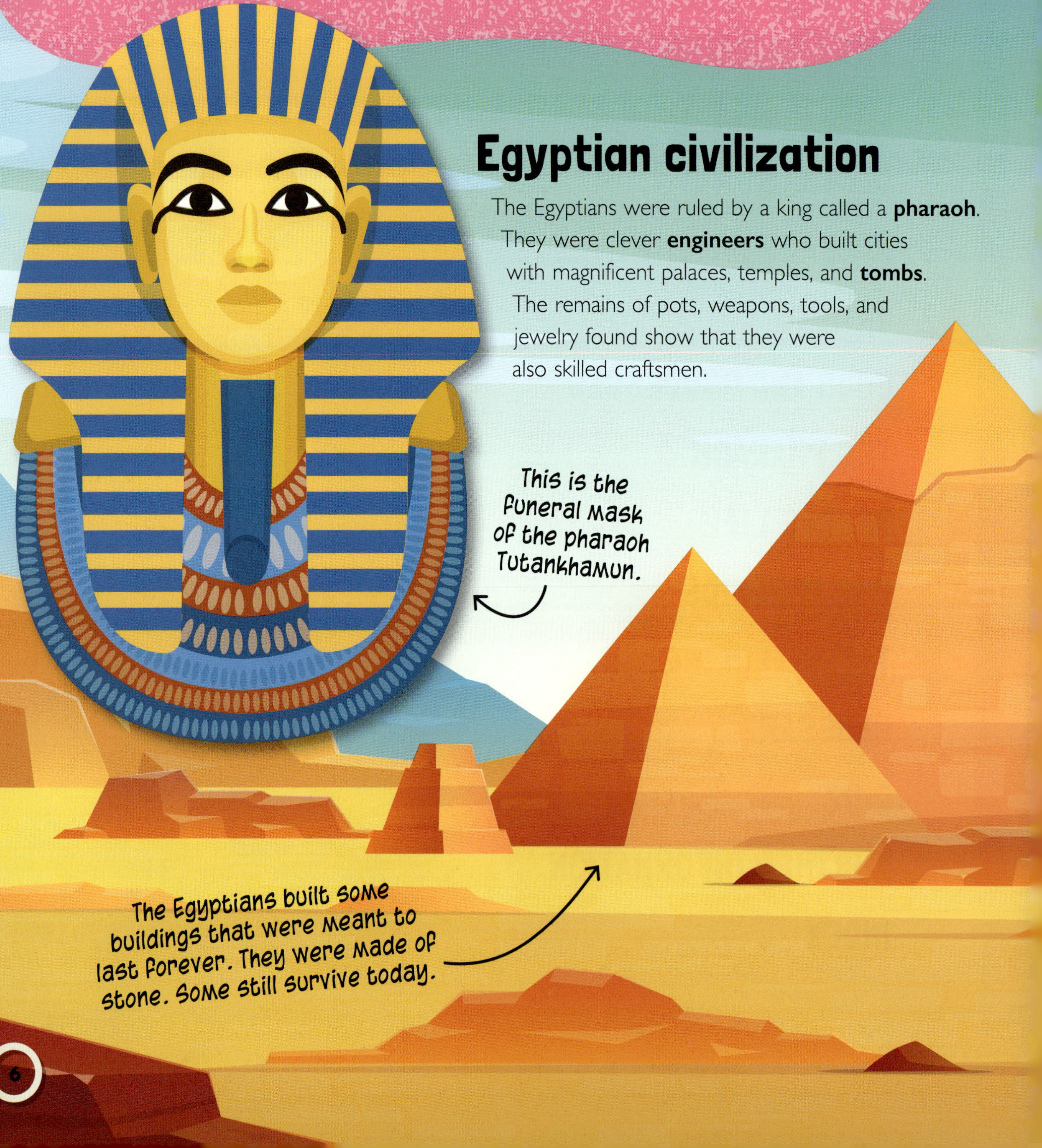

Egyptian traders traveled by ship to trade goods.

Trade

Egypt was a wealthy country. Egyptian traders sold their **goods** to Africa, the Mediterranean, and faraway India. They brought back exotic animals, ivory, timber, silk and perfume.

THE NILE RIVER

The Nile River is the longest river in the world. It runs through the North African desert and out into the Mediterranean Sea.

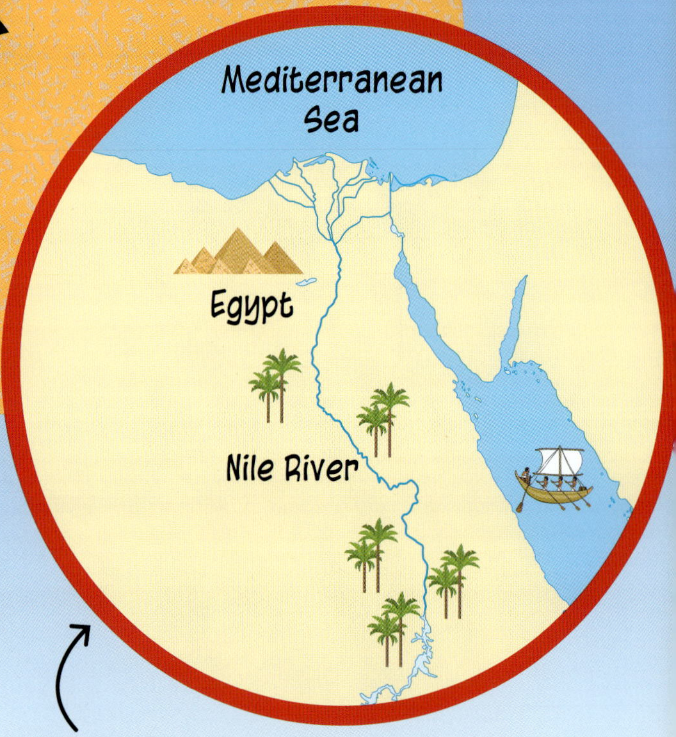

The Nile is surrounded by hot, dry desert where it hardly ever rains.

Floods

Snow melting in the mountains in the south floods the Nile every year in June. The floodwater leaves behind **silt**, which makes the soil good for farming.

Farming

The Ancient Egyptians settled along the banks of the Nile River and farmers planted crops in the rich soil. Their year was divided into three seasons called flood, crop sowing, and harvesting. Farmers cut **irrigation canals** to carry water from the river to the fields and villages as there was little rain.

The Ancient Egyptians used shadufs to lift water from the canals. Shadufs are still used today.

ACTIVITY

MAKE A SHADUF

You will need:

- **four sticks of dowel (three that are 8 inches [20 cm] long and one that is 12 inches [30 cm] long)**
- **string or twine**
- **modeling clay**
- **foil**

1. Tie together the three 8-inch (20-cm) dowels, 1 inch (2.5 cm) from one end. Spread them into a triangular frame. Press the ends into a modeling clay base.

2. Loosely tie the 12-inch (30-cm) dowel to the top of the frame, about 1.5 inches (4 cm) from one end.

3. Add a lump of modeling clay to make a counterweight to the short end.

4. Shape a bucket from foil. Hang it from the other end of the lever with a piece of long string.

5. Try it out. Pull the string down to fill the bucket with water. Push down on the weight to lift the bucket of water.

EGYPTIAN LIFE

Keeping cool and growing enough food to eat was an important part of Egyptian daily life.

Houses were made from mud bricks strengthened with straw and baked hard in the sun. You can still find houses in Egypt made like this.

Houses

Egyptian houses were built to keep out the heat. The walls were painted white to reflect the sun. Windows were small and high and vents in the roofs and walls trapped the cool north winds.

Nobles to slaves

Wealthy **nobles** served in the pharaoh's court. Educated **scribes** kept important records, and priests ran the temples. There were many traders and skilled craftsmen but most people were peasants who belonged to the landowners. There were also people who were enslaved.

Craftsmen made many different objects by hand, such as sculptures, jewelry, and tools.

Food

Rich soil alongside the Nile meant the Egyptians could grow lots of food for festivals and feasts. Bread and cakes were made from wheat and barley. Figs, dates, and grapes were either eaten fresh, or dried and stored, or made into wine. Egyptians caught fish from the river.

Egyptian paintings show people harvesting fruit and catching fish.

ACTIVITY

MAKE A FAN

You will need:

- **construction paper (white, gold, purple, and green)**
- **strong brown card stock**
- **scissors**

1. Cut out about 30 feather shapes (below) from white construction paper, about 6 inches (15 cm). long.

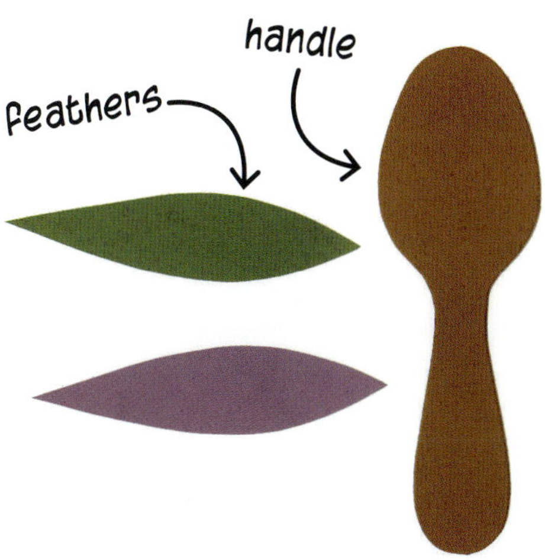

2. Cut out feathers in gold, purple, and green construction paper, three in each color.

3. Copy and cut out the handle (left) from strong brown card stock. Make it 8 inches (20 cm) long.

4. Stick the white feathers onto the back of the handle, adding the colored feathers to make a pattern. Use your fan to keep cool.

CLOTHES

Egyptian clothes were made from linen. They were light and loose for keeping cool in the heat. Men's kilts and women's dresses were often pressed into pleats. Farmers wore loincloths to work in the fields while children went naked in the heat.

Clothes were usually white, the natural color of the linen cloth, like the Egyptians are wearing in this wall painting.

Linen

Linen was made from the fibers of the flax plant. First the flax heads were removed with a type of comb. Then the stems were soaked, beaten, and combed until they were ready for spinning into thread.

Nets

Nets helped to protect linen clothes from wearing out too quickly. Soldiers wore leather nets over their kilts and women servants wore beaded nets over their dresses.

All of the beaded nets were made by hand.

ACTIVITY

MAKE EGYPTIAN SANDALS

The Egyptians wore sandals that were made from papyrus, a kind of reed that grows on the banks of the Nile.

Ask an adult to help you with this activity.

You will need:
- **thick carboard**
- **scissors**
- **hole punch**
- **brown ribbon**

1. Trace around your feet on a piece of thick cardboard. Mark two spots between your big toe and second toe. Mark a spot on either side of the heel.
2. Ask an adult to help cut out the thick cardboard soles and punch holes on the marked spots.
3. Tie two 4-inch (10-cm) pieces of brown ribbon in the holes by the heel, one in each.
4. Thread a 16-inch (40-cm) piece of brown ribbon down and back up through the holes by the toes.
5. Pull the ribbon so it is equal lengths and knot. To make the part that goes between your toes, tie the ribbon together again 2.5 inches (6 cm) along.
6. Tie the ends of the ribbons in bows around your foot. Finish the sandal for your other foot and try them on!

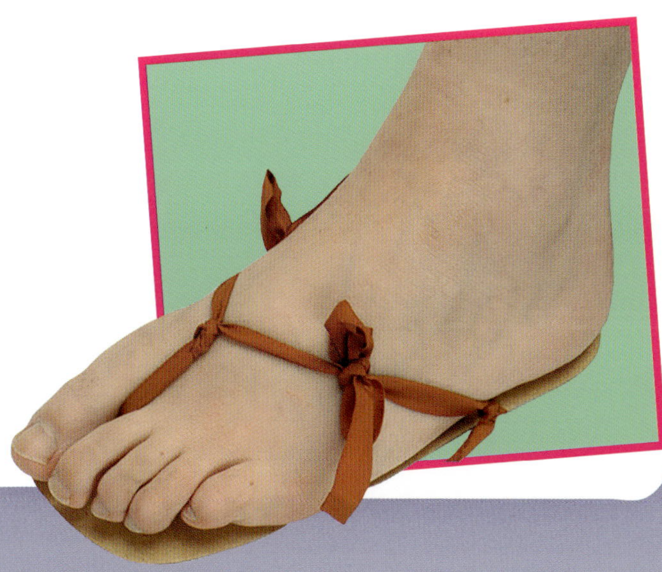

HAIR AND MAKEUP

Most Egyptians wore some jewelry. Ordinary people wore copper rings and **amulets** to keep away evil spirits. Jewelry for wealthy Egyptians was made of gold from Egypt's own gold mines. Collars, rings, ear studs, bracelets, and **anklets** were set with colorful semiprecious stones.

The woman in this ancient Egyptian painting is wearing a perfume cone on her head.

Wigs and wax

Egyptians wore long, black, braided wigs. A cone of scented wax worn on top of the head melted in the heat and trickled down the wearer's wig, making them smell nice.

Makeup

The Egyptians used mirrors, combs, tweezers, and makeup to achieve the style of the time. Colored minerals were ground into powder and mixed with wax to make black eye paint and red rouge for lips and cheeks.

Both men and women outlined their eyes with black makeup.

ACTIVITY

MAKE A DECORATED COLLAR

Craftsmen molded, beat, and carved metal into jewelry like this collar.

Decorated collars added richness and color to the plain linen clothes.

You will need:

- **large piece of card stock**
- **hole punch**
- **scissors**
- **paint, various colors**
- **drinking straws, various colors**
- **sequins**
- **ribbon**

1. Copy the shape of the collar. Make it as wide as your shoulders. Punch holes in the top as shown.

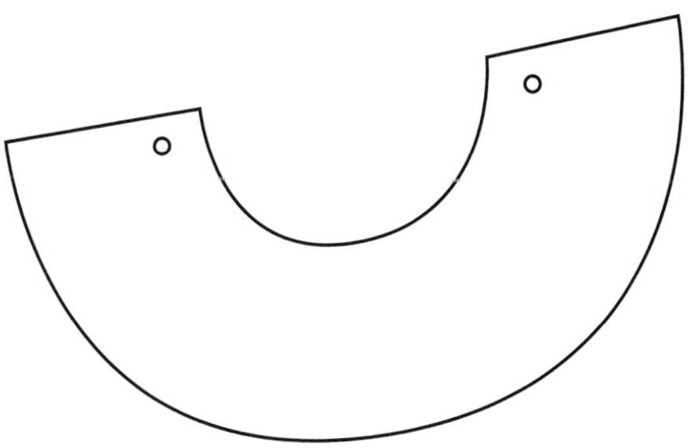

2. Cut colored straws into 1-inch (2.5-cm) lengths. Decorate the collar with alternate stripes of paint, rows of colored straws, and sequins.

3. Thread with ribbon and wear your Egyptian collar.

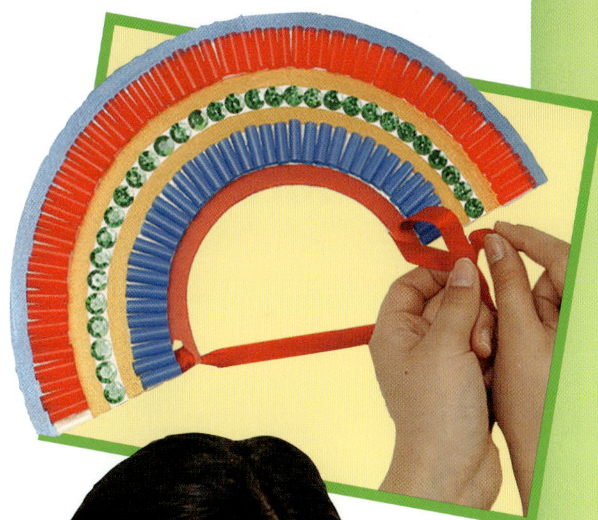

WRITING

The Ancient Egyptians wrote in hieroglyphs. Some of the words looked like pictures. For hundreds of years, historians could not understand the hieroglyphs.

The Rosetta stone unlocked the ancient secrets of the hieroglyphs.

The Rosetta Stone

In 1799, the Rosetta stone was found. The same words were written in three different languages: Greek, Demotic, and hieroglyphs. This meant that scholars could now translate hieroglyphs for the first time.

Scribes

Very few people could read and write hieroglyphs. There were about 700 signs to learn. Scribes started their training as young boys and took many years to learn to read and write hieroglyphs.

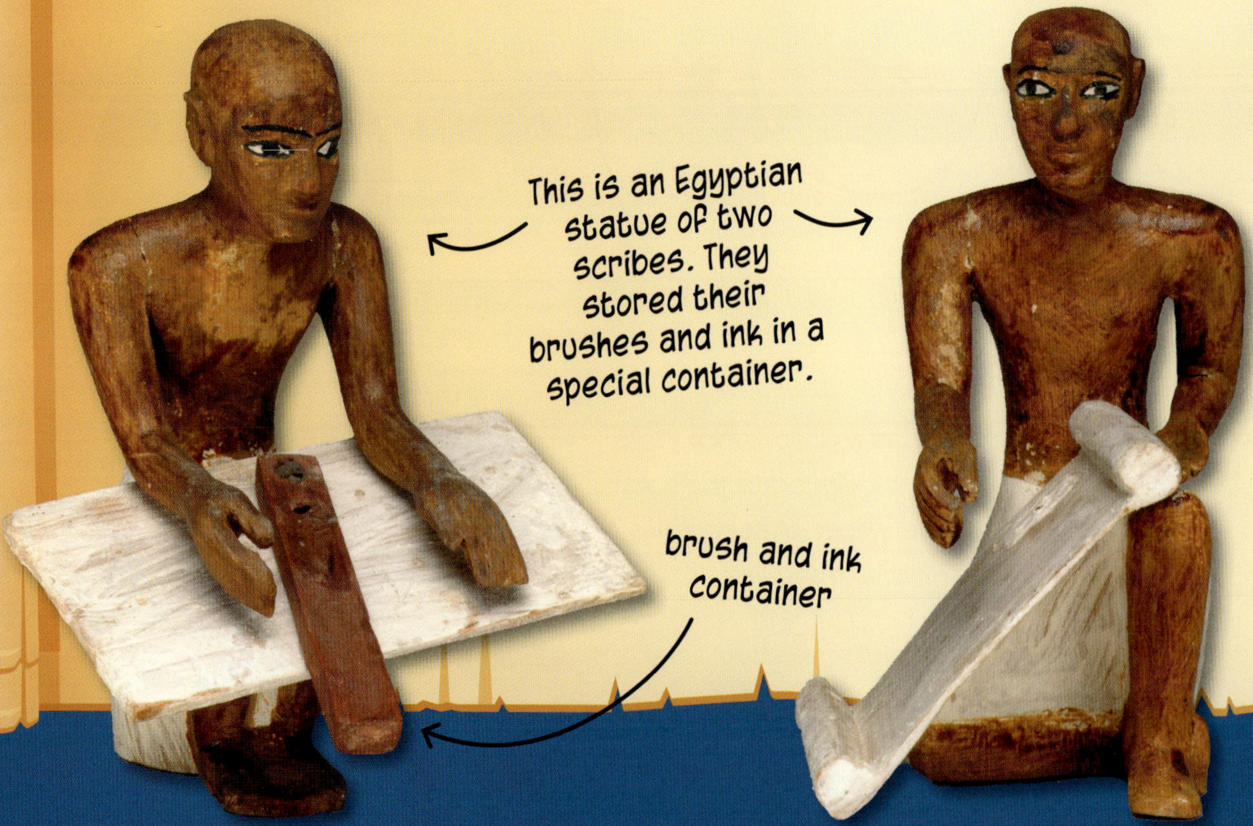

This is an Egyptian statue of two scribes. They stored their brushes and ink in a special container.

brush and ink container

Papyrus

Papyrus was a kind of paper made of pith from the stem of the papyrus reed. Strips of pith were laid criss-cross on a frame and flattened under heavy weights to make sheets.

Scribes wrote hieroglyphs on pieces of papyrus.

ACTIVITY

WRITE YOUR NAME IN HIEROGLYPHS

Hieroglyphs were either a whole word or a single letter. The name of a pharaoh was written on an oval **cartouche**.

You will need:

- **paper**
- **pens or pencils, various colors**

1. Write your name in hieroglyphs, using the key below.

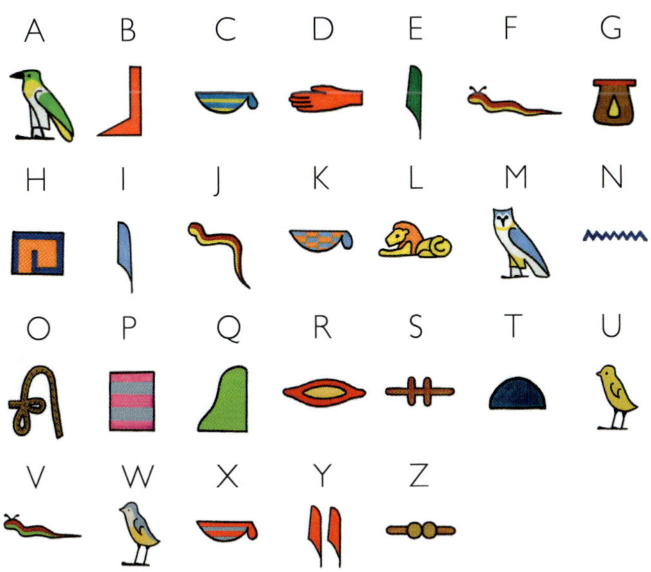

2. Design a cartouche around it, coloring it with vivid colors as if you were the king!

GODS AND GODDESSES

The Ancient Egyptians worshipped many hundreds of gods and goddesses. They believed in life after death and tried to make sure they would make it safely to the spirit world. Pharaohs went to a special place when they died called the "land of the gods."

The gods

Egyptians believed that the gods controlled human beings and all of nature.

Ra was the sun god and creator of men.

Thoth, the moon god of wisdom, had a curved beak of a sacred ibis.

Isis was the goddess of women and children.

Horus, protector of pharaohs, had a falcon's head.

Anubis was the jackal-headed god of death, rebirth and mummification.

Khnum was the ram-headed god of the Nile.

ACTIVITY

MAKE A HEAD OF THE GODDESS BASTET

Re's daughter, a cat called Bastet, was the goddess of the harvest.

You will need:

- **newspaper**
- **cardboard tube**
- **masking tape**
- **white glue**
- **water**
- **paint (green, yellow, and gold)**

1. Scrunch up some newspaper to make a fist-sized ball. Put it on top of a cardboard tube and fix it to the tube with masking tape.

2. Mix a little glue with water in a bowl. Tear up small pieces of newspaper and put them in the bowl to soak.

3. Shape two thick triangles from glue-soaked newspaper for ears and a strip for the nose. Fix with papier-mâché strips.

4. Cover the head with a layer of papier-mâché. Leave to dry thoroughly.

5. Paint your head dark green and make the eyes yellow. Use gold paint for earrings and a jewel on the forehead.

THE PHARAOH

The pharaoh was the king of Egypt. The Egyptians believed that the pharaoh was a god and that his wife was a goddess. A boy born to be the pharaoh learned to hunt, fight, and lead his army in battle. The pharaoh was also a high priest in the temple.

Ramses the Great ordered the building of the Abu Simbel temple. It has large statues of Ramses outside.

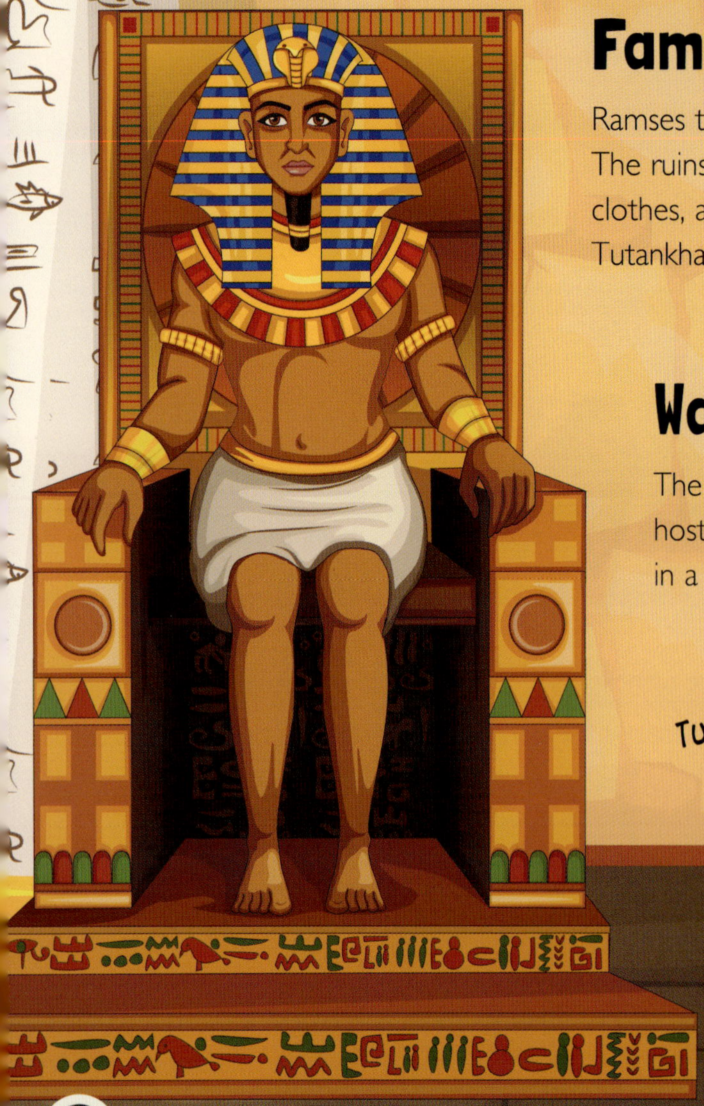

Famous pharaohs

Ramses the Great built many great buildings and monuments. The ruins of these can still be seen today. Similarly, jewelry, clothes, and weapons from the tomb of the pharaoh Tutankhamun tell us a great deal about Ancient Egypt.

War

The pharaoh went to war to protect his land against hostile armies or to take over another country. He rode in a horse-drawn chariot and carried a bow and arrow.

Tutankhamun rode into battle in a chariot.

A pharaoh had colored crowns for different occasions. He wore different-colored crowns in different parts of Egypt, and another color in times of war.

This is a statue of King Seti II. His crown was originally painted blue.

ACTIVITY

MAKE A PHARAOH'S BLUE CROWN

You will need:

- **card stock (blue and gold)**
- **scissors**
- **black marker**
- **gold paint, optional**

1. Copy and cut out the shape of the crown on blue card stock. Make it about the width of your head.

2. Decorate it with gold spots, a coiled cobra, and a golden sun disk.

3. Make a band of gold card stock to go around your head. Attach the blue crown and wear it.

TEMPLE LIFE

Egyptian temples were huge. They were built of stone because they were meant to last forever. Priests performed temple rituals, such as offering gifts to the gods. Only high priests and the pharaoh went into the inner temple. Ordinary people were allowed into the temple courtyard for festivals.

Around the temple

The temple gate was called a pylon. Statues of the pharaoh stood at the gate. Tall, thin **obelisks** carved with messages to the gods marked the point where the first rays of the sun fell. **Sphinxes** guarded the avenue in front of the temple.

The hour-watcher priest

The hour-watcher priest was in charge of making sure the temple rituals were carried out on time. By day, he kept time by the sun. At night, he used a water clock. Water dripped slowly from a hole in the bottom of a special container. It took an hour for the water level to drop from one mark to the next.

water clock from Ancient Egypt

ACTIVITY

MAKING A WATER CLOCK

Ask an adult to help you with this activity.

You will need:

- **large paper cup**
- **safety pin**
- **black paper**
- **white paint pen (or other pen that will write on black paper)**
- **water**
- **tall drinking glass**
- **waterproof pen**
- **clock or watch**

1. Make a very small hole in the base of a large paper cup with a safety pin (ask an adult to help).

2. Tape some black paper around the cup. Decorate it with Egyptian figures and hieroglyphs.

3. Fill the cup with water and suspend it in a tall glass.

4. How long does it take to empty? Mark the level of the water every 5 minutes with a waterproof pen on the inside of the cup.

THE PYRAMIDS

Egypt's great **pyramids** were tombs for some of the pharaohs and their families. Each pharaoh's body was laid in a chamber deep inside the pyramid where it was protected from the heat, and from robbers and animals. The burial chamber was filled with things the pharaoh would need in the **afterlife**.

The pyramid shape

The shape of the pyramid was built to look like the mound that rose from water at the beginning of time, as told in Egyptian **myths**. The sun god Ra stood on the mound's peak and called up all the other gods and goddesses.

The great pyramid

The great pyramid at Giza is about 4,500 years old. It was the tomb of King Khufu. The workers building the pyramid had no pulleys, only levers and rollers, to move two million blocks of stone. It took about 20 years to build one huge pyramid.

The sides of the pyramids look smooth but they are actually made out of many large stone blocks.

ACTIVITY

MAKE A PYRAMID

You will need:

- **yellow construction paper**
- **scissors**
- **glue or tape**
- **paints or pens for decorating**

1. Copy the pattern of a four-sided pyramid onto yellow paper and cut out. Include a flap on one edge.

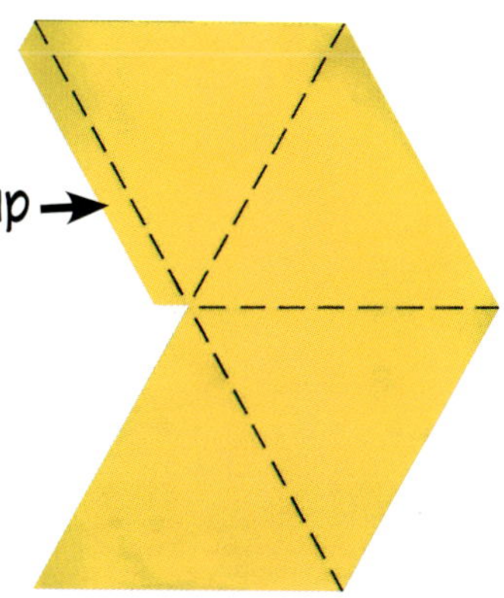

2. Fold along the dotted lines and attach the flap to form a pyramid.

3. Paint details on the pyramid. You could add a burial chamber in a small box inside.

THE AFTERLIFE

The Ancient Egyptians believed in life after death. They thought they needed their body in the afterlife so they took great care to preserve dead bodies. This was done by a process called mummification.

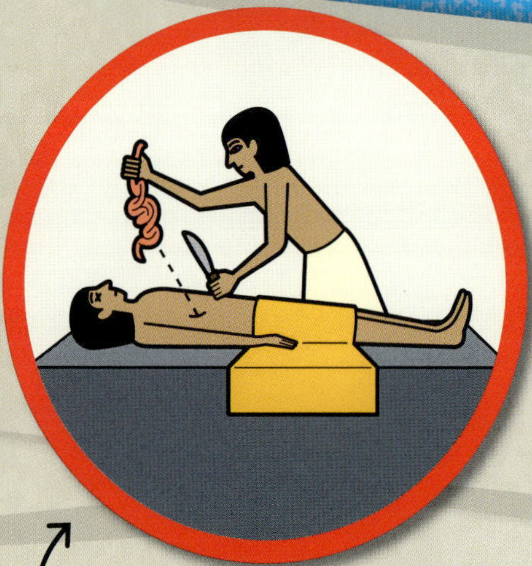

Mummification

Mummification was carried out by **embalmers**. The heart was left in the body.

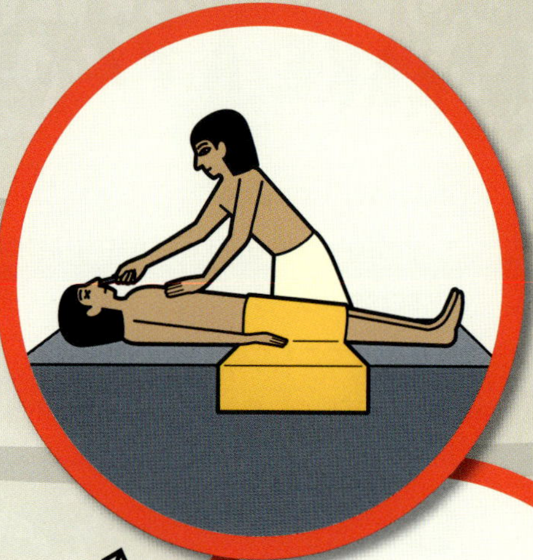

1 The lungs, stomach, intestines, and liver were removed, dried, and put in **canopic jars**.

2 The brain was pulled out through the nose with a hook.

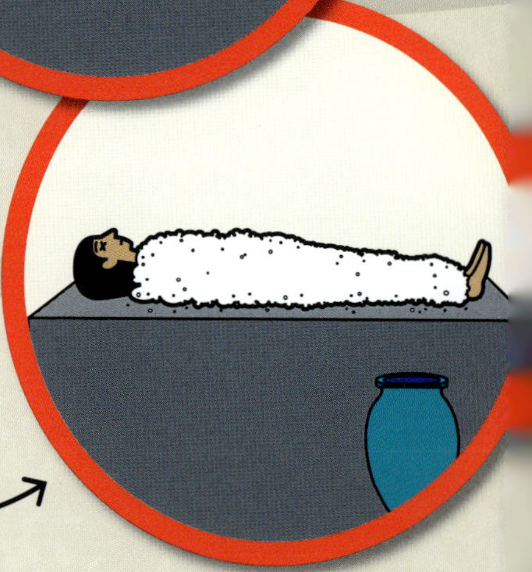

3 The body was dried, the face was decorated with makeup, and a wig was put on.

4 The body was rubbed with scented oil, covered in resin, and wrapped in linen.

Canopic jars often had decorated lids in the shape of gods and other important figures.

ACTIVITY

MAKE CANOPIC JARS

You will need:

- **four small glass jars**
- **paper**
- **pens or paints for decorating**
- **tape**
- **scissors**
- **orange peel**
- **small pink balloon**
- **dried noodle nest**
- **brown paint**
- **tea bag or coffee filter**
- **plastic wrap**

Hapi – baboon-headed god who protected the lungs.

Duamutef – jackal-headed god who protected the stomach.

Qebehsenuef – falcon-headed god who protected the intestines.

Imsety – human-headed god who protected the liver.

1. Copy the pictures of the four sons of Horus onto strips of paper to decorate the four glass jars.

2. To make the lungs, cut out shapes of lungs in orange peel and dry them out. For the stomach, blow up a small pink balloon and let out the air.

3. Make the intestines by painting dried noodles brown and dark red. The liver is a dried-out, used tea bag or coffee filter wrapped in plastic. Put each in a jar with its corresponding god on top.

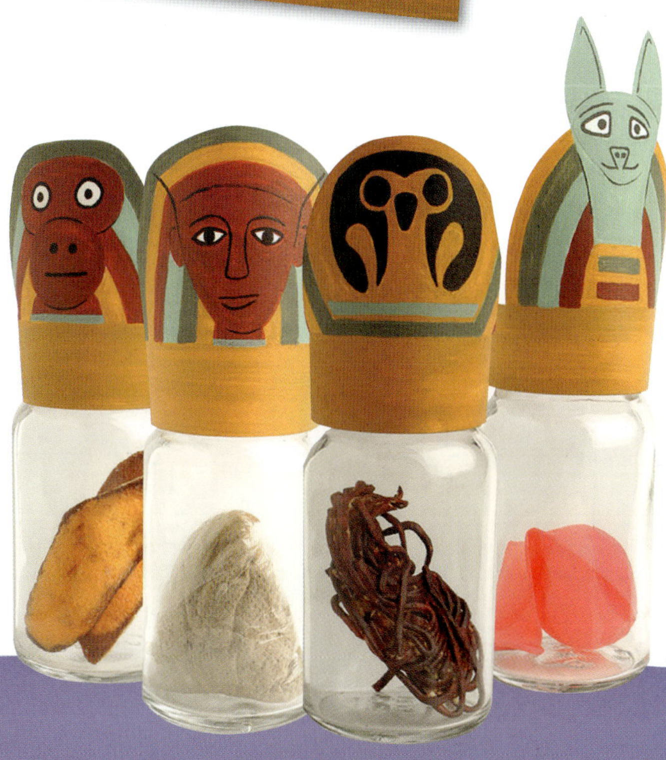

Glossary

afterlife

The afterlife is a life after death. The Egyptians believed they lived in another place after they died.

amulet

An amulet is a charm worn as protection against evil spirits.

anklet

An anklet is jewelry worn around the ankle.

canopic jar

A canopic jar is a jar used in Ancient Egypt to hold organs of the body.

cartouche

A cartouche is an oval shape that surrounds a pharaoh's name

civilization

A civilization is an organized society, usually based around a city.

embalmer

An embalmer is someone who treats a dead body to stop it from decaying.

engineer

An engineer is someone who designs and builds machines and buildings.

goods

Goods are things that are bought and sold such as food, cloth, and jewels.

hieroglyph

A hieroglyph is a symbol or picture used for writing. The Ancient Egyptians wrote in hieroglyphics.

irrigation canal

An irrigation canal is a ditch carrying water from a lake or river to fields where crops grow.

kilt

A kilt is a pleated, knee-length skirt.

linen

Linen is cloth woven from threads spun from the flax plant.

loincloth

A loincloth is a cloth tied around the hips and between the legs.

myth

A myth is an old story about gods and heroes in ancient times.

noble

A noble is someone with wealth and power in a royal court or government.

obelisk

An obelisk is a monument in the shape of a flat-sided pillar with a pointed top like a pyramid.

pharaoh

A pharaoh was a king of Ancient Egypt.

preserve

To preserve is to keep something from decaying or rotting.

pyramid

A pyramid is a shape with a square base and triangular walls. Some Egyptian royalty were buried in giant pyramids.

scribe

A scribe is someone who writes documents by hand. Ancient Egyptian scribes wrote in hieroglyphics.

silt

Silt is tiny pieces of mud or clay carried along by rivers. Silt helps to make soil rich for farming.

sphinx

A sphinx is a creature with a lion's body and the head of a man, a ram, or a bird.

tomb

A tomb is a grave, or a cave or a building that contains a grave.

Quiz

1. **Which river did the Ancient Egyptians live near?**
   a) Ganges River
   b) Congo River
   c) Thames River
   d) Nile River

2. **What did scribes do?**
   a) work on farms
   b) read and write hieroglyphs
   c) work in a temple
   d) take care of the pharaoh

3. **From which material were Egyptian clothes made?**
   a) linen
   b) wool
   c) papyrus
   d) silk

4. **What did Egyptian wigs look like?**
   a) short, gray braids
   b) hair of many different colors
   c) short, blond, curly hair
   d) long, black braids

5. **Which object helped historians understand hieroglyphs?**
   a) the Rosetta stone
   b) papyrus scrolls
   c) a shaduf
   d) the great pyramid

6. **Who was the Egyptian sun god?**
   a) Anubis
   b) Thoth
   c) Ra
   d) Isis

7. **Which animal did the god Horus have the head of?**
   a) leopard
   b) falcon
   c) cat
   d) crocodile

8. **Which weapon did the pharaoh use?**
   a) sword
   b) cannon
   c) spear
   d) bow and arrow

9. **Who was allowed into the inner temple?**

a) high priests and the pharaoh
b) no one
c) everyone
d) only the pharaoh

10. **Which body part was left inside a mummy?**

a) brain
b) stomach
c) heart
d) lungs

ANSWERS 1d, 2b, 3a, 4d, 5a, 6c, 7b, 8d, 9a, 10c

FURTHER INFORMATION

BOOKS

Millard, Anne. *The Ancient Worlds Atlas: A Pictorial Guide to Past Civilizations.* New York, NY: DK Publishing, 2023.

Redshaw, Hermione. *A Kid's Life in Ancient Egypt.* Minneapolis, MN: Bearport Publishing, 2023.

WEBSITES

Ancient Egypt

https://www.dkfindout.com/us/history/ancient-egypt/

Check out more about Ancient Egypt here.

Ancient Egypt Facts and History

https://kids.nationalgeographic.com/history/article/ancient-egypt

Read about Egyptian history on this site.

Index